D1562603

Your Personal Battle Plan

A Study Guide for The Unseen War

David Kortje

authorHOUSE®

AuthorHouse™
1663 Liberty Drive
Bloomington, IN 47403
www.authorhouse.com
Phone: 1-800-839-8640

First published by AuthorHouse 10/29/2009

ISBN: 978-1-4490-4152-6 (e)
ISBN: 978-1-4490-4151-9 (sc)

Library of Congress Control Number: 2009911220

Printed in the United States of America
Bloomington, Indiana

This book is printed on acid-free paper.

Acknowledgments

I really have enjoyed designing this study guide, primarily because there are so many who have come alongside to help.

First, there is Sandra, my wife, my partner, and my lover. She has encouraged me and given me the freedom to follow this sometimes crazy and always adventurous life that Christ has called me to.

I also owe a deep gratitude to my partner at Knight Vision Ministries, Jim. When no one else seems to "get" what I feel God has called me to, Jim always does. It is a true joy to find a man whose heart beats to the same rhythm.

Next are those who have boldly stepped out in faith and started small groups to study *The Unseen War* without any resources such as this guide. They became my beta test groups. They include Ed and Michelle and the small group that met in their living room, along with John, who hosted an international study over the Internet at www.RansomedHeart.net. The majority of our "intelligence briefings" came out of those groups.

I also owe a special thanks to my son Josiah, who never tires of updating our web site, packaging books to ship, and offering new ideas to reach others with this message.

Thanks also to Author House and my editor, Fran Lowe, for making me look and sound much more polished than I am, as well as the many others who support and encourage our efforts here at Knight Vision Ministries. I am very much aware that none of this would be happening without all of you.

Finally, thank you for the courage to walk out this life in Christ. We need you, and I need you. Fight well, my friends.

To the King,

David

Contents

Introduction

All that I really wanted to do was go camping. It was just two days before our annual men's hiking and camping trip in Colorado. Each year I head out to the Rocky Mountains with a group of men—some of my closest friends and some new ones—to experience the beauty and majesty of the high country. It's an opportunity for us to unwind, strengthen friendships, and step away from the noise of everyday life. These trips have produced some of my richest times with God as I am presented with the occasion to slow down enough to clearly hear His voice, as well as gain an opportunity to share and discuss this life in Christ with fellow warriors. This year I was especially excited because Caleb, my sixteen-year-old son, was coming with us for the first time.

Our plan was to leave at the crack of dawn on a Wednesday morning. So, crawling out of bed on Monday morning for what would be a short, two-day work week, I was genuinely excited. As I got dressed for the day, I grabbed my favorite wristwatch. It was dead. "Battery must have given out," I guessed. No problem— I just placed a different watch on my wrist. After running out the door and jumping on my Yamaha FZ-6 sport motorcycle bike to ride to work in the cool air of the morning (always my favorite part of any day), I hit the "start" button, and nothing happened. Again I tried, making sure the switch was on, but no go. Its battery was apparently dead as well. The truck would just have to do today.

Work began rather uneventfully at the clinic, where I am employed as a family practice physician—that is, until a chemistry machine of ours went on the blink. Not more than a few minutes later, as I was examining a patient, I literally saw my "working" wristwatch take its last tick and stop in front of my eyes. Then, as I walked out of the exam room, I asked my nurse to shoot an X-ray of the patient. She returned ten minutes later with the report that our X-ray machine was no longer working. It seemed as if something had gotten jammed, and she couldn't adjust the machine the way she needed to do it. "I've never seen it do anything like that before," she reported.

Now, at this point, my frustration was really starting to mount. I mean, my goodness, what else could go wrong?! The day finally ended, and I headed home. My plans were to charge the battery in my motorcycle and finish packing for our big trip. Upon entering the driveway, I was met by my thirteen-year-old son, Josiah. He and Caleb had been assigned to clear out some trees and brush on our property that day. "The tractor's broke," Josiah informed me. "The loader is stuck down and won't move. Oh, and it has a flat tire!" (I should have kept my mouth shut about what else could go wrong.) An hour or so later, the tractor was once again operational, and it was time to work on the motorcycle. Unfortunately, my battery charger didn't want to work either. I was finally able to get it to give a trickle charge, but I wasn't sure if that would be enough to get me to work in the morning.

And so, much later and considerably more frazzled than I had anticipated, I sat down to eat a late dinner with my wife. Finally, there was some good news for me: she has made her amazing fruit cobbler. So after the meal, ready for a little pleasure in my day, I hopped down the stairs to fetch the ice cream from the freezer. Walking into the utility room, my hopes of relaxation came crashing down as my bare feet stepped into an inch of water flooding our basement. That was the last straw! A combination of crying and screaming exploded from my lips. Water was already creeping into our basement carpet as Sandra grabbed a wet-vac, and I began trying to diagnose the problem. It took a few hours, but we were finally able to discern that the problem was coming from our water-source heat-pump air conditioner.

Unfortunately, that wasn't the end of our problems as we tried to accomplish our planning for this trip. Our water softener also went out that night, we slept with the windows open in ninety- degree weather, and my new cell phone was lifeless the next morning. Even as we finally got in the car on our way to Colorado, our "luck" began to rub off on my friend Chuck (who was driving us) as first his DVD player, then his GPS, and finally his camera all bit the dust.

You've had days like that too, I know you have—days when it just felt as if someone were out to get you or maybe to keep you from doing something. Maybe I'm just being paranoid. . .or maybe I know something. Jesus spoke clearly concerning these things when He said, "In this world you will have trouble. . ." (John 16:33), and "The thief comes only to steal, kill, and destroy. . ." (John 10:10).

I wrote *The Unseen War: Winning the Fight for Life* as a guide for those of us who are fighting these battles. It is so easy to just give up, lose heart, and cry "uncle." Since writing *The Unseen War,* the response has been amazing. Many hearts were encouraged, and many a warrior found the strength again to get up and fight. Yet more was still needed. Many wanted to walk through this book with friends—comrades that could help in the fight.

That is the purpose behind this personal battle plan you are holding right now. As a companion to the original book, it is designed to take you deep into the heart of the battle, to train and equip you for the adventure and life that our King holds for you.

Obviously, you can complete the questions alone in your own time, but let me encourage you to find some sisters or brothers to walk this out with. So much more can be learned and experienced as we do this together. In fact, much of the material and comments in this manual came from just such a group that I was a part of, and without them, *Your Personal Battle Plan in The Unseen War* would not have been possible.

As you work through this book, you will find some recurring themes. Allow me to offer some hints for these.

***

Theatre of the Round Table

Each chapter has at least one and sometimes two movie clips relating to the topic at hand. Some are from action movies, some from chick flicks, and some from comedies and dramas. First of all, let me just state the obvious: these are not "Christian" movies. They come from Hollywood, and as such, many of them contain content that is likely offensive to you and me. However, they also relay truths—truths that are more clearly seen and understood due to the talents and high production quality of the movie industry.

The apostle Paul used similar means in his day. We often find him quoting heathen poets and referring to pantheistic philosophies as he describes this Jesus to them. (See Acts 17:16-30.) So strongly did Paul believe in finding truth in all of this creation that in 1 Corinthians 3:21-22 he writes, "All things are yours, whether Paul or Apollos or Cephas or the world or life or death or the present or the future—all things are yours."

Thus, it is in that spirit that we offer you scenes presenting the truth in ways that we cannot. I warn you that some of these examples are graphic, while others have language or innuendos that may make you uncomfortable. Please understand my heart: I never want to present any stumbling blocks before anyone. I am confident that you can comprehend the meat of this message without them, so don't feel that you need to watch anything that doesn't set right with you.

However, if you do choose to use these examples in the group study, I believe they will leave some indelible impressions regarding just what the issues at hand are. I would suggest viewing them at approximately the place where they are found in the study guide, and then leave plenty of time for analysis and discussion of how they apply to our walk with Christ.

Messages from the King

Each page is followed by a blank page with the heading "Messages from the King." Perhaps the most important thing you can do as you work through this project is to take enough time out to pursue your King about what He would desire to convey to you. Use these pages to write what you hear or share your thoughts on a subject or a question. This is your book, and these pages are designed for your input.

Knightly Reading

Simply put, these are suggested Scripture references for your own personal study. Use them when and how our King directs.

Scouting Reports

I've added a few of these to offer a type of "heads up" about what may be coming against you during a particular section, or perhaps a suggestion on how to approach a specific area.

Intelligence Briefings

These are some of my favorite places in the book. They include quotes from other warriors. Some are famous, but most of them are just walking out this adventure as you and I are. This is a rich collection of wisdom and insight. Spend some time here and drink deeply of the wisdom of those who have gone before us.

***

Some final thoughts: This battle in which we are engaged is very real. We must not make the mistake of assuming it isn't or that we don't need to train and sharpen our combat skills. Take your time here, come back often, and I assure you that you will find your place in this great adventure . . . and you will never be the same.

Chapter 1
The Red Pill

You are about to enter into the most real thing that you have ever known. Much of what you thought you knew to be true will be challenged in the light of the Scriptures. If you have been beat up, torn down, and spit out, this study will offer context to those battles, as well as hope for walking through them and past them. If you are content with Sunday school, pot-lucks, and an occasional "Praise the Lord," this guide will honestly try to disrupt all of that—not that they are bad in themselves, but as a warrior you are called to so much more. If you are an experienced soldier in God's army, this battle plan will help provide clarity and direction as you engage in this great adventure. So I invite you to "take the red pill and enter the world of the Matrix— the world of fighting for your life."

Let's begin this with a quick reflection on your life up to this day. Surely everything in your life hasn't been a bed of roses. Share a time in your life when circumstances caused things not to work out the way you had planned.

With so much coming at me most of the time, I seldom have time to reflect about why bad things happen at all. I mean, my goodness, just this past week a storm flooded part of our property, our sump pump went out, an argument broke out among friends, another friend called to report in tears that his wife was leaving him, my motorcycle broke down, and I still haven't picked out a gift for Mother's Day tomorrow. Life seems to rush in on us at one hundred and eighty miles per hour, leaving us feeling dazed and confused about what all is exactly happening.

So what about you? Have you ever thought about your life in the context of warfare?
Why do you think we tend to minimize that aspect of life?

Messages from the King

Do you tend to view the battles that you fight daily as hassles mainly, perhaps frustrations, but "hardly the stuff of *Saving Private Ryan*"? Why do you think that is?

Scouting Report
Be careful here. Our enemy is likely trying to flank us at this point, coming in from our blind side, convincing us that this is paranoia and our time would be better spent in other pursuits.

Jesus entered our world as a baby—born in a manger, of all things . . . hardly the picture of power and authority and certainly not the way that I would take over enemy territory.

What do you think about the analogy of Jesus' entry into our world as an invasion?

Does that change your perspective of what Christianity is all about?

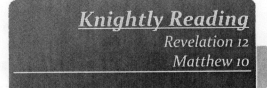

Knightly Reading
Revelation 12
Matthew 10

Messages from the King

Intelligence Briefing

It seems to me that any time we want to talk about the Enemy and his schemes, people want to label it to try and diminish it and get us to move to the place of, "Oh it's just bad luck" or hassles.

I believe we need to look at it for exactly what it is: war. We are at war. I don't think that if we were walking around with bullets zinging over our heads and talking about the Enemy's tactics with our comrades, we would be labeled as paranoid.

—Zachary

Okay, we all know that Jesus rose from that grave on Easter morning. He declares in Revelation, "I am the Living One; I was dead, and behold I am alive forever and ever! And I hold the keys of death and Hades" (Rev. 1:18).

If Jesus has already defeated Satan, what do you think the battle is about today?

The Theatre of the Round Table

I have called *The Matrix* "the gospel packaged for this generation." It is a powerful portrayal of the reality that we truly find ourselves living in. Let's begin with that "red pill" scene. It is found in chapters 8 and 9 (time code: 00:25:10—29:50). What analogies can you draw here that relate to the life our King, Jesus, has called us to?

In Matthew 10, as Jesus is sending His disciples out on their first field training exercise, He gives them some interesting instructions. He says, "Do not suppose that I have come to bring peace to the earth. I did not come to bring peace, but a sword" (Matt.10:34). Why do you think Jesus said, "Do not suppose"? What were they "supposing"?

Why do you think He gave this warning the very first time He sent them out?

Messages from the King

Intelligence Briefing
If you are courageous enough to
post your shingle as a Christian,
you're in the line of fire.
—John

Chapter 2
Gerry

The other shape,
If shape it might be call'd that shape had none
Distinguishable in member, joint, or limb,
Or substance might be call'd that shadow seem'd,
For each seem'd either; black it stood as Night,
Fierce as ten Furies, terrible as Hell,
And shook a dreadful Dart; what seem'd his head
The likeness of a Kingly Crown had on.
Satan was now at hand,. . .
                                        –John Milton
                    Paradise Lost, Book II, Line 667-675

So let's start this chapter with some poetry.

I am captivated by this quote from *Paradise Lost*. Milton does such a tremendous job of illustrating what cannot be described here: the very essence of evil, Satan. Don't rush this. Spend some time reading and re-reading this bit of poetry, and then comment on it.

What is John Milton saying about Satan? What does he look like, or what are his qualities?

Why do you think Milton saw a crown on his head?

Messages from the King

- John 12:31 Calls Satan the ~~God~~ ruler of this world. NIV Calls him the "Prince" of this world.
  Prince probably more accurate because a prince is under the King (Jesus) and can only act w/ permission of the King (Job).
- The Battle was won on the cross. D-Day won the war (war?) but there were still a few battles to fight. We've won, but there's still a few more battles to fight.

In the book I describe a time in my childhood when I ran into a bully. Eric Johnson is the fictitious name that I give to him, but it was a real incident. He was a troubled young man who went on to much worse things than making a couple of young boys eat dirt. However, the essence of the story is not so much about what he did but what it awoke in me when I began to realize that this is not a safe world.

What about you? Write out your first experience with evil, especially unexpected evil.

Why do you think the men of World War II called the enemy "Gerry"? Is there a advantage to identifying an enemy specifically and personally (Gerry), rather than just generally (the Nazis)? What is it?

— *To personalize their enemy.*

Satan attempted a coup of epic proportions that is described in Revelation 12, when he challenged the very throne of God. This is really quite incredible if you think about it for this is the same Satan who had sat on the holy mount of God, walked among the fiery stones, and knew first hand of the power, might, and holiness of God. He must have known that his chances were infinitesimally small, yet he tries to depose God from His rightful place as ruler of the entire universe. Discuss what possible motivation you think Satan might have had to take such a risk.

Knightly Reading
Isaiah 14
Ezekiel 28

Messages from the King

Consider the following passages:

> *How you have fallen from heaven, O morning star,
> son of the dawn! You have been cast down to the
> earth, you who once laid low the nations! You said in
> your heart, "I will ascend to heaven; I will raise my
> throne above the stars of God; I will sit enthroned on
> the mount of assembly, on the utmost heights of the
> sacred mountain. I will ascend above the tops of the
> clouds; I will make myself like the Most High."*
> (Isa. 14:12–14)

> *"You were the model of perfection, full of wisdom and
> perfect in beauty. You were in Eden, the garden of
> God; every precious stone adorned you: ruby, topaz
> and emerald, chrysolite, onyx and jasper, sapphire,
> turquoise and beryl. Your settings and mountings were
> made of gold; on the day you were created they were
> prepared. You were anointed as a guardian cherub,
> for so I ordained you. You were on the holy mount of
> God; you walked among the fiery stones. You were
> blameless in your ways from the day you were created
> till wickedness was found in you. Through your
> widespread trade you were filled with violence, and
> you sinned. So I drove you in disgrace from the mount
> of God, and I expelled you, O guardian cherub, from
> among the fiery stones. Your heart became proud
> on account of your beauty, and you corrupted your
> wisdom because of your splendor. So I threw you to
> the earth; I made a spectacle of you before kings."*
> (Ezek. 28:12b–17)

What do these sections of Scripture tell us about our enemy and his
motivations?

Messages from the King

Intelligence Briefing

Why do we have such a hard time admitting that we have a real enemy who wants to destroy us? I'd say that most of us are hesitant because once we admit that we do indeed have an enemy, we have to accept the responsibility for it. We then must choose whether to resist him or surrender to him.

—Allan

Hollywood, the Renaissance, and even our churches and places of worship have deeply influenced our understanding of the heavenly beings, angels and demons. Some of this is good; however, much of it is misleading, to say the least. How have your preconceived ideas of them affected your understanding of the power and fierceness of our enemy?

The Theatre of the Round Table

There are two clips that would be immensely helpful as we try to understand our enemy. The first is from chapter 30 of *The Lord of the Rings, Fellowship of the Ring* (time code: 02:04:30-02:09:02) as the Fellowship confronts the Balroc (an ancient evil from the mines of Moria). Next, watch chapters 12 and 13 from *Amadeus*, (time code: 00:51:23-00:58:30), and pay attention to the hatred of Salieri toward the young and talented Mozart.

One of the most dangerous and serious mistakes that soldiers can make in battle is to underestimate their enemy or take their strength for granted. Do you think that we sometimes take Satan too lightly? What advantage would that give him?

Messages from the King

Intelligence Briefing
Yes, we have victory in Christ because of Him
and His actions. We are heirs to the Kingdom
of Heaven. We must never, ever forget,
however, that there is someone in our world
who seeks to steal that victory away from us by
leading us to a place of apostasy.
—Jim

Chapter 3
Paradigm

We need to begin with a shift in our thinking: a paradigm shift. We need to begin looking at the battle for what it really is, not just the curtain that has been pulled over our eyes to blind us from the truth.

In chapter 1, I referenced Jesus' words to His disciples in Matthew 10:34, "Do not suppose that I have come to bring peace. . ."
What have you been "supposing" about this life that Jesus has called you into?

> *Or suppose a king is about to go to war against another king. Will he not first sit down and consider whether he is able with ten thousand men to oppose the one coming against him with twenty thousand?*
> *(Luke 14:31)*

What have you been supposing of the enemy?

What does the world suppose is going on here?

Share what you have been taught in church or the news media about what is wrong with the world and what is needed to "fix"it.

Messages from the King

Let's get specific about Satan now. He has been portrayed as everything from a cute little menace to the dark side of God, equal in power but pursuing evil rather than good. Many dismiss him as either a myth simply used to explain the pain in the world or an evil so strong and so powerful that we should avoid any mention of his name. He has been worshipped, bargained with, laughed at, and associated with everything from rock 'n roll to poltergeist experiences, from epileptic fits to agricultural diseases.

So what about you? What have you heard or been taught about Satan?

What do you personally believe about who Satan is?

The Theatre of the Round Table

Rent the HBO miniseries *Band of Brothers* and watch the sixth episode entitled *Bastogne*. Discuss the determination of these brave young men, freezing cold in a foxhole, as they fight to stop the Germans from gaining a foothold in this small Belgium town.

Messages from the King

Intelligence Briefing

More and more the land of "hopelessness" seems to take on more inhabitants who wish they could turn back once entered. Equally the promised "land of hope" is being fought for by so few on a daily basis.

--John

Footholds are those little things—those seemingly insignificant failings that we all experience and never really deal with until they mushroom into a disaster: The Internet pictures that we just glance at occasionally, the anger for that one who harmed us which we rather enjoy dwelling upon, or our tendencies to cover our pain with chocolate, whiskey, or fantasy. An acquaintance once actually told me that it was okay to keep a bath towel or two from the hotel where we stayed, because the hotel builds some loss into our room rates!

Name some of the footholds that Satan has tried to gain in your life or those around you.

I wrote in *The Unseen War* that "Satan continues to offer the Tree of Knowledge instead of the Tree of Life" (p. 29). Have you ever seen that temptation play itself out in your life or in the circles that your travel in—when Satan offers something that looks enough like a greater understanding of God and the universe that you begin to wonder why God didn't show you that? Explain.

Is there a difference between the "Knowledge of God" and the "Life in God"?

What is it?

Messages from the King

Intelligence Briefing

Sin in any form will hurt many others besides the one who did the sinning. I have been married twice. My first marriage ended in divorce because my ex wife stepped out on me, which hurt me badly. Through God I forgave them both, but before I did that I did the same thing to my present wife, and it was because I hadn't forgiven my ex. I let Satan use that lie to do the same thing to this marriage.

—Dave B

Tozer writes that "the visible becomes the enemy of the invisible, the temporal of the eternal" (*The Pursuit of God*, p 54). So much of what we see seems so real and so final that we are often left with this feeling that there is no more—that we just need to accept life as it is and make the best of it.

How has Satan assaulted your everyday life by telling you that "this is all you get; there is no greater reality."

Satan's first temptation of Christ was to "feed that need—that hunger." I love that the Scriptures reveal how Jesus was tempted in that way because it is so. . .human. It reminds me that Jesus really was tempted in every way, just as I have been. It also reminds me of what a significant temptation that is—that deep desire we have to satisfy our appetites whenever they call.

Where have you observed Satan use that temptation in your life and in the lives of those you know? In other words, where have you observe the drive to "feed that need," which leads to a divergence from the path that God has laid out?

Knightly Reading
Matthew 4:1-11
Luke 4:1-13
Genesis 3:1-13

Messages from the King

Intelligence Briefing
Once you have made the world an end, and
faith a means, you have almost won your man.
—C. S. Lewis
The Screwtape Letters, p. 35

I'm one of those "take control" kind of people. I absolutely hate it when nothing is happening because I start feeling nervous, uncomfortable, and unproductive. Subsequently, I will go out of my way to get something—anything—going. Sometimes that is a very good thing. When there is a gathering or a party and no one is interacting, I will usually go out of my way to get things started. Likewise, when I feel like our ministry is stalling, I will begin brainstorming for ideas of what we can do differently. However, there is also a very dark and dangerous side to that. Often it is God who is "slowing" us down, trying to teach us to walk in His timing or perhaps trying to save us from heartache or failure. It is during those times that I am particularly susceptible to Satan's suggestions to "find a better way."

How about you? Have you ever felt that you were in a desert—that God was holding out on you and it was time to take matters into your own hands?

What is the danger of making the "end" (the very thing that God has called you to do) the goal? *In other words, why is it dangerous to justify the means (doing whatever it takes, regardless of how you do it) in order to accomplish the goal? Is it possible that God is just as interested in the process of getting there as much as just getting there?*

Why do you suppose that it is so hard for us to trust God to take us there in His time?

Messages from the King

Intelligence Briefing

My favorite part of the chapter is p. 33,
where David proposes that maybe the
most dangerous part of the battle is ahead.

—Zachary

Chapter 4
No Ordinary Guy

Who am I? You sure you want to know? The story of my life is not for the faint of heart. If somebody said that it was a happy little tale ... if somebody told you that I was just your average ordinary guy, not a care in the world ... somebody lied.
—Peter Parker in Spiderman

Peter Parker begins to understand something about himself as his character develops in the hit movie *Spiderman*, but this has not always been the case. Early in the story he sees himself more as a cockroach than a spider-man. He has failed with his friends, failed with his family, and even failed with the girl.

Now let's be honest here. How do you view yourself? What are the words that you have heard in your own mind concerning who you are?

Have you ever considered that maybe those words were coming from your enemy?

"Created in the image of God" implies so much about who we really are. We are created in His beauty, with His love for adventure and the story. We are created with passion—passion for people, passion for the battle, and passion to love sacrificially. We are created with authority and even with a creative nature. In what ways does the nature of God manifest itself in your life?

How do you see it manifested in the deeds of men and women?

Messages from the King

Intelligence Briefing

It seems that most believers do not see themselves as extraordinary, at least not in God's eyes. We think that God has passed us over and only a select few get noticed. I'm not talking about salvation; I'm referring to significance.

The term "where my eyes were uncovered" was brought out by Scripture itself, "You have stolen my heart..." (SS 4:9). I guess I still have yet to come to full terms with the meaning here. Me? Stealing God's heart! I'm ugly; at least that's what I was told growing up.
—John

God commands Adam, His created man, to "fill the earth and subdue (*kabash*) it" (Gen.1:28). Using your own words and vernacular, discuss your understanding of the meaning of the Hebrew word *kabash*. What type of emotions would you expect this type of authority to produce in Satan after his failed attempt to seize that authority?

What emotions does it produce in you as you consider this authority that was bestowed on you by your creator?

> *T*hen God said, "Let us make man in our image, in our likeness, and let them rule" ... So God created man in his own image, in the image of God he created him; male and female he created them. God blessed them and said to them, "Be fruitful and increase in number; fill the earth and subdue it ..."
>
> (Genesis 1:26-28)

Paul offers us a glimpse of who we truly are in 1 Corinthians 6:2-3. Arguing that we should be competent to judge in disputes between believers, he states: "Do you not know that the saints will judge the world? ... Do you not know that we will judge angels? " WOW! Think about that statement for a while, and let it sink deep into your heart.

Now consider this: How must God view us if He has appointed us to judge the world and yes, even angels?

Messages from the King

Scouting Report
Be on your guard for the propaganda and lies of your enemy here. Those thoughts that you are feeling, —those thoughts that whisper in your ear, "That's not true of me; that can't be true of me; look at me, I am nothing'"— are directly of Satan, denying the very work of Christ in you. You must not agree with them.

Paul tells us that something radical happens to us as we receive Christ. We are told that Jesus Christ, the God of the entire universe, is now living in us. It was, and is, an absolutely insane statement. We are literally possessed by God. You realize, don't you, that in any other context they would put you away in a mental institution for believing such a thing?

> *...The mystery that has been kept hidden for ages and generations, but is now disclosed to the saints. To them God has chosen to make known among the Gentiles the glorious riches of this mystery, which is Christ in you, the hope of glory.*
> *(Colossians 1:26-27)*

So what *does* it mean to you to have Christ living in you?

What does that say about what is truest about you?

After reviewing my suggestions on p. 42 of *The Unseen War*, think back over the last few weeks. Can you identify those times when you were trying to pursue God or some area of restoration, perhaps in a relationship or personal area, when literally "all hell broke loose"? Do you really think that was just bad luck, or might there be someone who is afraid because you are walking forward in that area of your life?

Messages from the King

Intelligence Briefing

He fears that in the end he will lose: That most of us, or at least enough of us, will prove God's point that we are worthy. That good is the better way, and that by God's commands there is life. That we will choose to be followers of God and not turn against God as he did. That God's army will grow and his will weaken and he will be left forever banned from that which he once sought to rule. He fears the power of our choice.

—Virginia

How about some fun and fantasy: Imagine for a moment that yesterday you received a registered letter from the attorney for Bill Gates, the founder of Microsoft. He explains that new evidence proves you are actually the long-lost heir of Mr. Gates, and as such, all that he has is yours.

> *For you did not receive a spirit that makes you a slave again to fear, but you received the Spirit of sonship... Now if we are children, then we are heirs - heirs of God and co-heirs with Christ.*
>
> *(Romans 8:15, 17)*

How would you live differently? Would your mortgage or credit card payments worry you as much as they do now?

How would you react differently the next time that your car breaks down?

In Bible times, it was the son who was the heir—the one who inherited all that was the father's. According to Romans 8:12-17 and 1 Corinthians 3:21-23, what has God given us in Christ?

Knightly Reading
Psalm 8
Song of Songs

Messages from the King

Zephaniah 3:17 says, *"He will take great delight in you, he will quiet you with his love, he will rejoice over you with singing."* Many believers have a hard time seeing God as thrilled, even giddy, over us.

Who do you think has the most to profit from our doubt of God's intentions for us?

After reviewing this chapter, put into your own words why Satan hates you so. What words of condemnation has he used recently on you?

Messages from the King

Chapter 5
Flesh

We are embarking into the very heart of the battle now. It is no longer theory and strategy-planning but rather blood and guts and noise and chaos. This is the crucible in which we are tested, the critical turning point in any campaign worth its salt.

General George S. Patton, one of the icons and great leaders of World War II, once said, "Never let the enemy pick that battle site." What do you think he meant, and why would that be important?

> *But now that you know, [Satan's] tactics have changed. Now he wants to breathe apathy on you.*
> *The Unseen War, p. 48*

I shared my own story in *The Unseen War* of sitting in the back of the megachurch, just trying to escape some of the chaos that had become my life. You must understand, it wasn't as if I was trying to walk away from God; it was rather just the opposite. I was trying to stay close to God, just in a "safe" place. You see, I had allowed the Enemy to convince me that I didn't *need* to fight in this war—that it could just be Jesus and me living happily ever after. It was a lie.

I wrote that Satan wants you "to choose safety over adventure, peace over war, and comfort over conflict." What are some ways, or where are some of the areas, that you have seen him do just that?

Messages from the King

The story of Moses is a fascinating look at the contrast between following our calling in our own flesh and following it with our King. And so many of us have done this: We have tried to walk out our calling in our own strength.

So how about you? Have you ever, like Moses, tried to walk into your own calling, only to fail miserably?

What effect did that have on your desire to try again?

The Theatre of the Round Table

This week, let's watch chapter 19 from *The Lord of the Rings* trilogy, *The Return of the King* (time code: 01:01:09-01:06:23). It is the part in the story when Frodo, weary from the battle, chooses the ring and his part in the story over wisdom and the true battle.

Messages from the King

Intelligence Briefing
There is a life that is so rich and fertile, so strong and resilient, so wise and cunning, so pure and true, so simple and clear that it will touch the world in unforgettable ways.
--Gary Barkalow
Founder and Director of The Noble Heart

Gideon really asks the definitive question, doesn't he? After seeing his land decimated by his enemies, failing to see God move on behalf of the children of Israel, God's people, and faced with the reality that now all seems lost, Gideon asks, "If the Lord is with us, why has all this happened to us?" (Judges 6:13).

Likewise, we're asking, "Why hasn't God come through, why hasn't He fixed our country or our family, why hasn't He avenged our enemies, why do the innocent suffer, or for that matter ... *why can't I get a job!?* The scenarios are endless.

I've asked this question a thousand times. (I suppose that you have also.)

When?
   When have you asked, "Why has all of this happened to us?

Messages from the King

Scouting Report

I like to lift weights and have been on a fairly consistent schedule for the past three years. I used to do this all the time in high school and college; but once I got into the world, sadly, my time for exercise went by the roadside. It has been an enjoyable experience to rebuild muscle that I feared I had lost during those years in which I didn't exercise. In many ways, I think that I am in better shape than I was in high school and college. But with that gain in physical strength, I have discovered a flaw. There are times, because of my strength, that I tend to rely heavily upon my physical abilities rather than my spiritual relationship. For example, if things are kind of rough at home, no problem. I am in good shape; I can handle the extra load. The evil one, sensing this, has used this to his advantage. . . .

On occasion, I will substitute-preach at our local church. As I was preparing for my last opportunity (about three weeks ago now), I was running through the materials in our home office, and the words weren't coming to me like I thought that they should. I was growing increasingly frustrated and kept working harder and harder in a vain effort to make the words flow like I desired. After all, I knew the material that I was going to speak on very well —this should have been easier than it was. After several hours and a whole bunch of frustration, it finally dawned on me that I was working independent of my heavenly Father. With this revelation, I stopped what I was doing and began to pray. I went to bed, got up the next morning, and headed off to church. Everything went fine. . . .

As I was sitting between services caught somewhere between prayer and thought, I began to wonder about how typical this was for me. One thing is for certain: I must be mindful of how much my flesh dominates my actions.

—Jim

Messages from the King

King David was supposed to go to war that spring. After all, that is what he was—a warrior king. But instead he chose to stay home. However, in the comfort and solitude of his castle, supposedly away from the battle, a much more dangerous conflict ensued. As a result, so much was compromised and lost.

I know that you too have fought long, hard battles—perhaps like David—for years; and like David, it has worn on you. So let's list them. What battles have you fought long and hard at?

What are the fights that you wish you could just take a break from and stay home for a change?

> *Be strong and courageous.
> Do not be afraid or terrified because of them, for the LORD your God goes with you; he will never leave you nor forsake you.*
> *(Deuteronomy 31:6)*

So where *is* your heart now? What shape is it in?

Messages from the King

Intelligence Briefing

I too have wanted to hide for years: holding on
to rotten things, dwelling on past failures, and
listening to the voices that tell me nothing is going
to change. Though all along, something inside
kept me begging God for it to change. It was
my personal book of revelation, I suppose. The
flesh took one last monumental assault, and all I
thought I wanted I took—only to find out it was all
lies. Flesh can never deeply and lastingly satisfy.
It's like living only in dreams, with reality coming
upon us when we wake.

—Peter

It's time now: time to step back into the battle, time to take your place at the right hand of your King. After all of Gideon's questions and fears and self-doubt, we finally find him ready to step onto the field: "Early in the morning, Jerub-Baal [that is, Gideon] and all his men camped at the spring of Harod" (Judges 7:1).

So what about you? Write out on paper where you have been taken out, where you have compromised, failed, or just plain had enough.

Knightly Reading
Judges 6
Luke 10: 38-42

And then, if you dare, pray this prayer:

Jesus, the battle has been hard. I have tried; I have given all that I know to give. My spirit has been willing, but my flesh has been weak. Forgive me for the times that I have given in, when I have laid down my sword in favor of the sofa. Forgive me for hiding in winepresses and even churches. I renounce those ways. I choose the one thing needful: I choose You. Restore me, rescue me, and release me from my own prison that I may follow You into the heart of the battle once again.

Messages from the King

Chapter 6
Light

*"But what if ... what if there is more to me than what I see?
The Oracle had said I had the gift, but what if it isn't just
about talent and training? What if there really is more to me,
more to me than I am seeing now?"*
–The Unseen War, p. 57

You too are more than what you see. You may not believe that right now. That's okay, for that is exactly what you would suspect, if in fact we have an enemy who is trying to hide the truth from us. But not believing it (or wanting to believe it but fearing it is not true) does not need to preclude us from looking at the question and honestly asking God to reveal to us the truth of the matter.

The Theatre of the Round Table

Watch the subway battle scene from *The Matrix* (chapter 33 at time code 01:54:16 – 01:58:27). Why was Thomas Anderson's training both important for the battle but also not enough? Why is it not enough for us to simply learn about our faith?

Messages from the King

Intelligence Briefing
Who am I? Am I this roly-poly body that is
prone to decay—this form once shaped from
the clay that will one day seek a home once
more with the clay?
If that is what you see, then you are blind.
—Virginia

"Do you hear that, Mr. Anderson? That is the sound of inevitability." The words of Agent Smith are the words of our enemy, for he has spoken them to each of us multiple times. What are the areas in your life where you have heard those words of inevitability that have said, "It is inevitable that you will never. . .be a good enough parent, find your place in the world, kick that habit, become that person God has for you,

_____. . .(you fill in the blank)?"

> *Therefore we do not lose heart. Though outwardly we are wasting away, yet inwardly we are being renewed day by day. For our light and momentary troubles are achieving for us an eternal glory that far outweighs them all. So we fix our eyes not on what is seen, but on what is unseen. For what is seen is temporary, but what is unseen is eternal.*
> *(2 Corinthians 4:16-18)*

Have you ever felt like you were on the brink of losing heart?

What might Paul have meant when he told us to "fix our eyes not on what is seen, but on what is unseen" (2 Cor. 4:18)?

Like Neo, could there be something that is truer of us than the world that we see around us every day?

Messages from the King

Here's an exercise for you. Grab a highlighter (one of those yellow felt-tip pens that you used in college to mark the "important sections" in your textbooks). Now sit down with your Bible and open it to the Book of Ephesians. With marker in hand, highlight every place that Paul uses the words "in Christ," "in Him," or "through Him." Now read through all the highlighted areas again. Share your thoughts.

In your own words, who are we in Christ?

In Paul's letter to the Romans, as he discusses and explains this new life that we now have in Christ, he urges us to count ourselves dead to sin (Rom. 6:11). He tells us that we do this in the same way as we received Christ—in other words, by faith. Yet, we still sin. What do you suppose Paul was trying to convey to the believer?

Look at the following chapter, Romans 7. In this passage Paul personifies sin, speaking of it as if it was something other than who he was. (See verses 8, 11, 17, and 21.) What did Paul believe about who he was now in Christ?

Messages from the King

Intelligence Briefing

To be honest. . .I don't think "the church"—
that's us—really believes what it means to be
"new creatures in Christ." If we did, we would
conduct our lives differently.
—Ruth

Find Ephesians 1:17 in your Bible. It is a beautiful snapshot of the inner prayer life of Paul. According to this prayer, what is essential to knowing Jesus?

What is the difference between wisdom and revelation? Why do you think we need both?

> *If you have faith in Christ, you are in Christ and He is in you, just as Christ was in the Father and the Father was in Him.*
> *—The Unseen War, p. 62*

The Russian philosopher Nicolai Berdyaev wrote: *"We find the most terrible form of atheism, not in the militant and passionate struggle against the idea of God himself, but in the practical atheism of everyday living, in indifference and torpor* [inactivity]. *We often encounter these forms of atheism among those who are formally Christians."*

Unfortunately, if I'm honest, I must admit that so much of my life is lived within the confines of this "practical atheism," which results in my denial of the very life that Christ died to offer me.

How would your life be different if you lived as if the same power that raised Jesus from the dead was available and working in you?

Messages from the King

Intelligence Briefing

It seems to me the answer is simply that my heart is GOOD! For me, this changes everything. Jesus Christ came on my behalf, and He has transformed my heart. This is the "new creature," as I understand it. When I fall to sin, it is NOT the real me. My heart is good: the reason I know this to be true is that when I sin, it grieves me. If my heart was not good, I would not care.

—Zachary

I really appreciate the analogy that Watchman Nee used of the three men: Fact, Faith, and Experience. It explains so much about my own experience and the result that it had on my faith as I've looked at the "failed" Experience and concluded that Faith must not work.

Have you ever made a similar mistake of looking at Experience to define your Faith, rather than looking at Fact? How did that turn out?

Nee points out that "If we resort to our senses to discover the truth, we shall find Satan's lies are often enough true of our experience." What do you think he meant by that? (See quote on pp. 63-64, *The Unseen War*.)

If we can't resort to our senses to discover truth, how do we discover truth?

Finally, he states that "if we refuse to accept as binding anything that contradicts God's Word and maintain an attitude of faith in him alone, we shall find instead that Satan's lies begin to dissolve and that our experience is coming progressively to tally with the word" (*The Normal Christian Life*, pp. 78-89). It sounds so easy, and yet we find so many other things to put our faith in than just "him alone."
List some of those "other things" that you put your faith in.

Now consider this: Who has the most to gain as you trust in those things?

Knightly Reading
Ephesians 1-3
Romans 6-7

Messages from the King

Intelligence Briefing

... laying down our own selfish desires and allowing Him to lead us in the desires He has for us. Once we begin to do that, we begin to experience freedom and life like we have never known. It's not easy. It's often scary. It's an adventure chasing the dreams that God has placed in our hearts and having the courage to take that first step. Like Benaiah, we are chasing the lion down into a pit on a snowy day.

—Michael

We often then find ourselves in agreement with our enemy over the meaning of these experiences. How might those agreements sabotage our very understanding of our position in Christ?

Jesus says in Matthew 17:20 that if you have faith as small as a mustard seed, nothing will be impossible. I don't know about you, but that does not seem to be the reality of my life. I mean, *nothing* will be impossible? Sometimes almost *everything* seems impossible. How do you come to terms with verses like that?

The truth, of course, is that we live in an unseen world—one whose truth has been hidden from us, just as Neo lived in a world that was not what it seemed. The "trick" is not to "make" the spoon bend; the trick is to understand that "there is no spoon." What are some areas right now where you can choose fact over experience and you too can say that there is no spoon?

Messages from the King

Chapter 7
Ears

*Teach me your ways, so that I may know
you and continue to find favor with you.*
(Exodus 33:13)

We actually talk about hearing from God all of the time. "I'll pray about that decision" implies that we are hoping to hear a response as a result of our prayers. Likewise, the ever-popular adage, "God seemed to close that door," suggests that there is some type of communication channel open between us and Him. So, what types of difficulties do you tend to encounter as you try to hear from God?

What have your experiences been in this area?

And what if we don't hear? What if we walked through our entire lives without hearing from God? What if we made all of our decisions and choices solely on the basis of chance or maybe experience? What if we just went wherever we pleased without first checking with our King? What do you think are the dangers of that?

Messages from the King

Do you believe that God is actively participating with His Creation? Explain.

Jesus tells an incredible story in John 10. He describes this corral, or pen, in which sheep live. He then explains that there is an enemy of the sheep who tries to gain access to the sheep by any way possible, regardless of the "rules." This enemy is a thief whose only purpose is to "steal, kill, and destroy" (v.10). However, there is another man, Jesus explains. He doesn't slither in; instead, He walks in through the gate. In fact, He *is* the gate. Read that parable again in John 10:1-18. Describe the relationship that the Shepherd has with His sheep.

Scouting Report

Communication is so central in any battle, (especially ours, when so much is at stake) and the interpretation of it is so important that it will be opposed by the full force of Hell itself. We must be careful not to make any agreements with our enemy here. Jesus says plainly that His sheep hear His voice.

Messages from the King

Intelligence Briefing
"Get into the habit of saying, 'Speak, Lord,'
and life will become a romance (1 Samuel 3:9).
—Oswald Chambers
My Utmost for His Highest, Jan 30

While Jesus is meeting with His disciples for the final time before His crucifixion, He begins putting all of the pieces together and offering some last-minute instructions. He explains to them that He is the only true way to God; in fact, He tells them that He *is* God. He also begins to describe the third member of the Godhead, the Holy Spirit, who "will teach you all things" (John 14:26).

He then explains what our relationship with Him should be like, comparing it to a branch that has been grafted onto a vine; and that we can only accomplish anything through this relationship (John 15:1-8). Jesus goes on to explain that we will be hated and opposed, just as He was hated and opposed (John 15:18-16:4).

And then in John 16:12, Jesus says that He has much more to say to us. What do you think He meant by that? Why would He want us to know that?

The Theatre of the Round Table

There is a very funny but also all-too accurate scene in the movie *Bruce Almighty* *(chapters 5 and 6, time code: 00:19:16-00:25:16)* in which Bruce is angry at God for not speaking to him. Do you think it is possible to miss the voice of God because of the "filter" through which we are listening?

What specifically in your life is making it difficult to "practice His presence," as Brother Lawrence describes?

Messages from the King

Intelligence Briefing
If there were only one sense we could take
into this war, it would be our sense of hearing.

—John

Okay, so let's get practical here. If we hold any hope of hearing God, we must know where to listen. One of the first places to start is within our own hearts, the dwelling place of God. In order to do this, though, we must recognize the very presence of Christ in those hearts. When the Old Testament prophets pointed toward this time when Jesus would restore all things, they gave us some very impressive promises about what would happen to our hearts:

> *"I will give them a heart to know me"* (Jeremiah 24:7).
> *"I will give them singleness of heart"* (Jeremiah 32:39).
> *"[I] will assuredly plant them in this land with all my heart and soul"* (Jeremiah 32:41).
> *"I will give them an undivided heart"* (Ezekiel 11:19).
> *"I will give you a new heart"* (Ezekiel 36:26a).
> *"I will remove from you your heart of stone and give you a heart of flesh"* (Ezekiel 36:26b).

Why is it important to listen to your heart as you seek the voice of God?

Of course, no one said that this would be easy. There are many other "voices" out there. According to pages 74 and 75 of *The Unseen War*, how do we discern the voice of God as opposed to our own voice or the voice of our enemy?

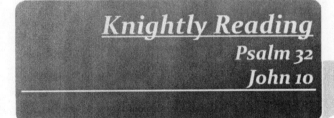

Knightly Reading
Psalm 32
John 10

Messages from the King

Studying the Bible is certainly useful and helpful, and in some circumstances, it can draw us closer to God. Yet we must not confuse *studying* the Word with *listening* to the Living Word; there is a vast difference. Have you ever heard the Word of God speak to you?

What was that like and how was that different than say… memorizing the missionary journeys of Paul?

Perhaps another way of looking at this question would be to ask: Why did God give us his Holy Bible? Was it simply because He wanted to show us how things happened—much like a history book explains the Civil War to us? Or did He offer it to us as a collection of stories and examples of Him communicating and interacting with His people, while at the same time inviting us into that interaction, that story?

> *For the word of God is living and active. Sharper than any double-edged sword, it penetrates even to dividing soul and spirit, joints and marrow, it judges the thoughts and attitudes of the heart.*
>
> *(Hebrews 4:12)*

At the end of chapter 7 in *The Unseen War*, I discuss the Parable of the Persistent Widow. It is a difficult teaching to understand in the light of an all-loving, all-knowing, and all-powerful God.

Why do you think that God values tenacity as we seek Him?

Messages from the King

Intelligence Briefing
"Are you really listening... or are you
just waiting for your turn to talk?"
—Robert Montgomery

Chapter 8
Together

First of all, what type of personality do you have? Do you tend toward being introverted (gaining energy from being alone) or extroverted (gaining energy from being with others)?

In order to walk closely with a band of fellow comrades, much will be required of us. While our close friends can offer their support and encouragement, they are also aware of our truest selves—with all of our insecurities and inconsistencies. So, let's be honest: how easy is it for you to share your deepest needs and failures with others?

Scouting Report

We are entering the best and the worst of the battle. Our fellow warriors can either save us or destroy us. Before going any further, it is imperative that we know within the deepest part of our hearts who we are in Christ; for we must not approach others with the need or expectation for them to answer that question for us.

Messages from the King

Intelligence Briefing

For me, "stubbornness" and "self-sufficiency"
were factors keeping me from the unity I once
had with some family members and my church
at the time. "Resentfulness" also drove a
wedge between us. Even so, I thought that
these "strengths"—as I used to think they
were—got me through many rough spots.

—Ruth

I share the hiking story up Mount Yale at the beginning of this chapter. Who do you think risked the most: Was it me, for asking my friend if I could carry his pack, thus threatening my plans and individualism; or was it Chuck, for allowing another man to help him?

What were those risks? (In other words, what did each have to lose?)

To think I did all that,
and may I say, not in a shy way -
Oh no. Oh no, not me.
I did it my way.
-My Way
Frank Sinatra

While I was listening to the radio in my car a few months ago, the DJ shared the results of a recent survey asking what is the most popular song sung at funerals: it is *My Way* by Frank Sinatra. Why do you think that is?

What does that say about our society as a whole?

There is something very romantic about doing it "my way"—something that speaks to the heart of my need for significance and independence. How has that thinking influenced your Christian walk?

What might the source of that "need for significance and independence" be?

Messages from the King

Intelligence Briefing
O who will walk a mile with me
Along life's merry way?
A comrade blithe and full of glee,
Who dares to laugh out loud and free
And let his frolic fancy play,
Like a happy child, through the flowers gay
That fill the field and fringe the way
Where he walks a mile with me.

And who will walk a mile with me
Along life's weary way?
A friend whose heart has eyes to see
The stars shine out o'er the darkening lea,
And the quiet rest at the end o' the day –
A friend who knows, and dares to say,
The brave, sweet words that cheer the way
Where he walks a mile with me.

With such a comrade, such a friend,
I fain would walk till journey's end,
Through summer sunshine, winter rain,
And then?—Farewell, we shall meet again!

A Wayfaring Song
Henry van Dyke

What about the Church? In what ways do you see that same self- sufficiency, that "I did it my way" mentality, showing up among Christians? The Scriptures teach that you will know the source by looking at the fruit. What fruit have you observed from this Lone Ranger mentality? What is that telling you about its origins?

The Theatre of the Round Table
We have a couple of clips to choose from as we explore the walking out of this battle with comrades. Chapter 15 of *Gladiator* (time code: 01:21:21 – 01:29:12) is a somewhat gruesome (but very realistic) scene of what happens when we choose to fight together. Another can be found in chapter 49 of *Lord of the Rings, Return of the King* (time code: 02:34:03-02:36:13). As you watch either of these, consider the barriers to fighting together that each one faces and what the consequences may have been had they chosen to go it alone.

'Then God said, 'Let *us* make man in *our* image, in *our* likeness ...' " (Genesis 1:26, emphasis mine). It is interesting that the Old Testament text uses the plural "us" and "our" in this passage of the Godhead discussing the creation of man.

Why do you think God, in creating us in his image, created us to need and desire relationships?

Messages from the King

First Corinthians 12:14-18 offers a snapshot of a truly dysfunctional church family as one of the parts tries to separate itself from the whole. What happens when one member desires to shine without the others?

What does this passage and the verses following suggest was God's plan for His bride, the body of Christ?

Most of us really struggle with asking for help, usually in a couple of very conspicuous areas. For example, I find it rather easy to ask someone to assist me in choosing the latest clothing styles, such as which shirts match which pants, but I find it very difficult to ask a friend to lend a hand with repairs around the house. When is it hardest for you to call for help?

Greater love has no one than this, that he lay down his life for his friends.

(John 15:13)

This verse that Jesus speaks is a bit of an enigma to those of us living in the western world. Living within the safety of our nation's borders, we are seldom called to literally give our lives for anything.

So how do we do this? How do we "lay our lives down for our friends"?

Messages from the King

Acts 2:42-47 is the classic narrative that explores the relationships of the early church. How might the results of the battles that you face every day be different if your local fellowship lived as that community of early believers lived?

Try this, for the next few weeks: text, Twitter, or e-mail a few friends with every struggle that you face, no matter how small (The car won't start, my stomach hurts, the kids are impossible, another bill just showed up …). Don't ask for a reply or advice, just lay it out there. See what happens.

Knightly Reading
Acts 2
Romans 12
1 Corinthians 12

Messages from the King

Intelligence Briefing
All my life God has blessed me with
the gift of friendships—some great and
long-lasting, others not so great that
didn't last. But with each one of them I
have felt blessed because I have walked
away with something from all of them.
—Joanne

Chapter 9
Surrender

I probably have a dozen projects in my shop just waiting for me to complete. They all sounded like such a good idea at the time; but as difficulties or conflicts arose, like so many others, they were left undone and placed in the corner. So, how about you? Recount your life. What are some of the projects or passions that you have quit on before they were finished?

What were the circumstances surrounding you at the time that made you feel like quitting was the best option?

> *Never, never, in nothing great or small, large or petty, never give in.*
> *–Winston Churchill*

As I wrote about my experience in the back of that megachurch, I related those words that I spoke to Satan: "I'll back down if you'll back down; just leave me alone." What specifically was wrong with that thinking, and why is that a dangerous thing to do?

From what we have learned about our enemy, do you think that he would ever honor such a truce?

Messages from the King

Intelligence Briefing

Perseverance is the underlying factor in our battles, which in itself is an ever ongoing process, even to our last breath. One battle calls us to another, and on and on.

—John

It certainly appears that events didn't quite turn out for John the Baptist as he had planned; he died at the hands of an evil ruler. That last discourse his disciples have with Jesus is very intriguing. What do you suppose Jesus meant when He said, "Blessed is the man that does not fall away on account of me" (Luke 7:23)?

Are there areas where those words could apply to your life today?

Paul writes that "God's gifts and his call are irrevocable" (Romans 11:29). So much is implied in those words: God has a specific call on your life, it is a good call worthy of walking out, and He was not mistaken in giving it to you. In fact, God is so confident that this is what He truly created you for that He will never remove that call on your life.

What are those callings and gifts that you have sensed in your life in the past?

In light of that Romans passage, do you believe God still has that call on your life, perhaps refined somewhat in the fire?

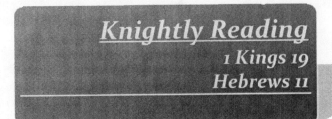

Knightly Reading

1 Kings 19

Hebrews 11

Messages from the King

Intelligence Briefing
God has a plan for all of us. And even through
adversity that plan doesn't change much.
—Ruth

Luke 9:51 states that "as the time approached for him to be taken up to heaven, Jesus resolutely set out for Jerusalem." The King James Version says "he stedfastly set his face to go to Jerusalem." What would it look like for you to "resolutely set out for Jerusalem"?

For that matter, what would your Jerusalem be?

Are there any issues or barriers that are standing in the way of your "resolutely"?

What are they?

What would it take to remove them?

Are you willing to remove them?

Scouting Report

Perhaps more than any other part of the battle, this one calls for wisdom and revelation from our King, for our enemy will surely try to convince us that those roadblocks are just "closed doors"; and sometimes, honestly, they are. So it behooves us to walk closely with God, to listen intently, and to lay down our own agendas in favor of His leading. One of the most useful tools here is to follow the blocked path forward to its fruit and ask ourselves this question: Is it self-glorifying or God-glorifying?

Messages from the King

Intelligence Briefing
And when the night is cold and dark
You can see, you can see light
'Cause no one can take away your right
To fight and never surrender, to never surrender.
—Never Surrender by Corey Hart

Have you ever felt like God was holding out on you or maybe not answering your prayers quickly enough?

Can you identify any lies that Satan throws at you during those times? List them.

What is in danger of not being accomplished for the kingdom if you choose to listen to those lies?

The Theatre of the Round Table

This week let's look at *The Pursuit of Happyness*, chapters 10 and 11 (time code: 00:38:13-00:45:45). It is a fun and heartwarming scene of a man down on his luck presented with an opportunity to fulfill a dream. Pay particular attention to how he deals with the forces and situations that are opposing him.

One of my favorite things about David in the Psalms is just his guttural honesty with God. He doesn't edit his prayers or soften his tone to sound more pious than he is, but rather he just allows his heart to cry out to his Lord. Psalm 142 is a beautiful example of one of these prayers as David admits that his enemies are too strong for him. What do you think God's response is to that kind of a prayer?

Messages from the King

On page 99 of *The Unseen War*, I wrote that "Perseverance is one of the greatest acts of faith that we can express. It pronounces with finality that we do trust His plan for our lives." As we walk out these daily battles and as days turn into years and victory perhaps seems further away than ever, explain your thoughts on what exactly it is that we are declaring when we choose to stay in the battle versus stepping out of this unseen war.

Read the story of Elijah at Mount Horeb in 1 Kings 19. What were the lies that Elijah was hearing and believing?

> Never yield to
> force; never yield
> to the apparently
> overwhelming might of
> the enemy.
> —Winston Churchill

God is calling you to "Go back the way you came" (1 Kings 19:15). If you dare, write out on a separate sheet of paper those areas in your life when you have, like Elijah the great prophet, declared that "I have had enough, take my life, I give up."

Now take that list, together with the lies that Satan has spoken, before your King. Ask Him to forgive your lack of faith. Ask Him to heal your wounds and give you your heart back. Then take your list and burn it in a fire, flush it down the toilet, or shred it. Declare to your enemy that you will "never, never, in nothing great or small, large or petty, give in!" Never!

Messages from the King

Intelligence Briefing

However, I hear another voice, a softer but more persistent voice that tells me to keep going—one that tells me that there is more to come.

--Allan

Chapter 10
Wounds

What deep wounds ever clos'd without a scar?
-Lord Byron
Childe Harold

There is something about that quote from Lord Byron's poem that haunts me.

Childe Harold is the story of a young man who has become so disillusioned with his life of comfort and pleasure that he goes on a quest for adventure in foreign lands. Like the "childe" (which incidentally was a title given to a young man who was training to be a knight), I too have sensed that there must be more to life than just my own personal gratification, yet I have also come face to face with this reality about wounds.

And so, let's consider that quote. What all do you suppose Lord Byron was alluding to in that?

The beginning of chapter 10 was one of the hardest but also most liberating chapters that I wrote, as I was able to spell out—while at the same time, release—some of the pain associated with the loss of Joshua. Read through that narrative again, and list all of the people and circumstances that led up to that fateful day when we lost him. Understand that our purpose here is not to assign blame but rather to identify with the complexity of such a wound.

Messages from the King

Intelligence Briefing

I heard once at a conference that scar tissue is like Super Glue®: it holds everything together but it also cannot ever be removed.

—Jim

We've all seen the news stories of combat veterans coming home from a war. We've heard the stories of brave men and women losing their limbs, eyesight, or even brain function from a roadside bomb or a sniper's bullet. Discuss the emotions that you have felt as these real-life stories have unfolded before you through the nightly news.

What thoughts come to mind concerning the soldiers, their families, or the enemy that wounded them?

What has been your experience concerning the reaction of the Church (Christians) to other Christians with wounds?

How has it been similar or different from your reaction to the news stories of combat vets?

Why is that?

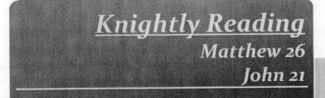

Knightly Reading
Matthew 26
John 21

Messages from the King

Intelligence Briefing

The gospel I signed up for was the "give your heart to Jesus and your life will be wonderful" one. Well, for me it was immediately intense warfare because I was leaving the Mormon church, and my bride was staying. Then my brother, who was my business partner at the time, began showing signs of addiction and mental illness. We lost the business shortly after that. So for me, I was confused about what it meant to be a Christian.

—Zachary

Review the contrasting yet similar stories of Judas and Peter described on pages 107-109 of *The Unseen War*. It is both hopeful and tragic as the Scriptures paint the choices and the responses to those choices of these two followers of Jesus. Discuss what you believe could have been at the root of Judas' despairing and Peter's weeping.

The Theatre of the Round Table

Chapters 31 and 32 (time code: 01:45:00-01:51:20) of *Batman Begins* would be good to view at this time. In this clip, even Bruce Wayne (Batman) realizes that he is not invisible as his enemy strikes with a ruthless plan. Bruce has a choice: will he receive his wound as the final judgment on himself, or will he listen to the wisdom of his old friend, Alfred?

I write that Judas made a judgment on God, not on himself (p.108). Let's unwrap that statement just a little. What do you suppose that I was alluding to?

Are there perhaps events in your own life when you have made similar judgments on God under the guise of a condemnation of yourself?

Messages from the King

I love that story of Jesus approaching Peter once again on the lake, on his terms in the area of his reality, and inviting him to breakfast. Consider the question that our Lord asks Peter: "Do you love Me?"

What do you suppose Jesus was trying to accomplish when He asked Peter this question three times?

I write that "it is often at the very heart of our quest that the deepest wounds come" (bottom of page 110). Why do you think that is?

Scouting Report

This is a critical area to pay special attention to— this area of deep and recurrent wounds. What exactly is it within us that our enemy is trying to extinguish by these strategic strikes? If we look carefully, we will often find a pattern, and that pattern will likely reveal much of our place in the battle—the place that our enemy fears we may take.

Why do you think that King David was able to immediately turn from his rebellion and once again follow God with abandonment rather than offer a time of self-imposed penance?

Messages from the King

Intelligence Briefing

The Enemy absolutely despises me, because he's aware of God's plan for my life here on earth. His attacks take on that vicious/subtle play in my life.

—John

It's time to get real again. List your wounds: those caused by others, those caused by circumstances or acts of nature, and those caused by your own failures.

Now take that list to the foot of the cross. Ask Jesus if His wounds were sufficient to heal your wounds. Ask for forgiveness for not believing that they were. If you aren't sure, find an army medic who knows the King, and ask him or her to lead you through the healing of those wounds. Don't worry about the scars or even the pain left by the wounds; those may stay. The question at hand is whether the wound has disqualified you from the battle. (Hint: the answer is no.)

Messages from the King

Chapter 11
Retreat

If you are like me, that word "retreat" just doesn't leave a good taste on your tongue. We are taught that retreat is a sign of weakness and defeat, hardly the stuff of winning battles, yet any war-trained general will tell you that often it may very well be the retreat that saves the troops so they can win the war.

Can you identify any times in your life or in the lives of those you know that the better part of valor would have been to retreat?

Did you or did they retreat or not, and what were the consequences?

> *"Everything is permissible for me"–*
> *but not everything is beneficial.*
> *"Everything is permissible for me"but*
> *I will not be mastered by anything.*
> *(1 Corinthians 6:12)*

The account of Saul facing the Philistine army in 1 Samuel 13:1-14 really hits home with me: wanting God to rescue me, wondering where He is while at the same time holding onto my own agenda and fears.

What do you suppose were the thoughts that were going through Saul's mind as he watched the Philistine army growing and his own men deserting him?

Messages from the King

God really unleashes His anger on Saul for not waiting for Samuel and the blessing. In the context of great failures, this one seems rather minor in comparison, yet the consequences were most severe, because Saul lost his kingdom, his future, and the anointing of God.

Why do you think God was so upset?

From this account, would you say that God is more concerned with us doing His work (fighting his enemies) or walking with Him in intimacy? Why?

The Theatre of the Round Table

I'm thinking that a little levity might be good about now, so drag out your copy of *Monty Python and the Holy Grail*. (You know you've got one.) Watch chapters 21 and 22 (time code: 01:08:53-01:14:17) as they face the vicious rabbit at the entrance to the Cave of Caerbannog. The scene really does a nice job, in a fun way, of demonstrating our reluctance to listen to wisdom, our underestimation of our enemy, as well as our need to rely on things beyond our understanding (the holy hand grenade).

What is the danger in thinking "the battle itself is the goal?" (bottom of p.117).

Messages from the King

I wrote in the book that there is a significant part of the battle that is primarily for our benefit. What do you think I meant by that?

What might that benefit be?

Think back on your own battles and the arrows that you have taken personally. In what ways has God fathered and trained you through the fires?

> *This calls for patient endurance and faithfulness on the part of the saints.*
> *(Revelation 13:10)*

Sometimes I feel like the most impatient person on the face of the earth. I want things done my way, and I want them done now.

Have you ever experienced a time of wanting to "take matters into your own hands" in order to accomplish what seemed like a worthy cause? Explain.

How exactly did that work out?

Messages from the King

Intelligence Briefing
It certainly seems one of the preferred orders of
the day for the Enemy is busyness. It appears
to be working in my life. We are inundated with
whatever that is that would work in distracting us.
—John

Jesus speaks to the church in Thyatira in Revelation 2: "I know your deeds, your love and faith, your service and perseverance, and that you are now doing more than you did at first. Nevertheless, I have this against you: You tolerate that woman Jezebel." (vv.19-20).

Many have compared the American Christian culture to this church at Thyatira. Would you agree or disagree? Explain your answer and the similarities or differences that you see.

Jesus has called us to life in Him. I'm not sure that I understand exactly what all that means, but in order for us to walk in that kind of life with Him, it is imperative that we hear His voice clearly and consistently.

So, how is that different than just doing deeds in His name?

Our enemy is quite experienced at taking believers off-track and leading them into ambushes. He has, after all, been at this for some time now. It would be good for us now to begin identifying from where those attacks may come and discussing what our escape routes might be.

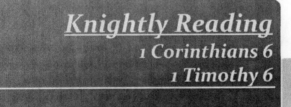

Knightly Reading
1 Corinthians 6
1 Timothy 6

Messages from the King

Two things seem evident from this chapter on retreat. First, we must know what it is that God has called us to. Second, it is imperative that we are in regular communication with the Father in the midst of walking out that call and be willing to change course on a moment's notice.

Let's practice now. Get away for a time by yourself, and ask God these two questions:

What do You have for me?

How am I to proceed today?

Messages from the King

Chapter 12
Boot Camp

Okay, I can't be the only one who has tried to wing it. What similar experiences have you had to my NASCAR debut—when you really wanted to do something, but you just didn't have the necessary training?

What was the outcome?

The Theatre of the Round Table

Few scenes paint a clearer picture of the disciple's need to trust the master's training than chapters 15, 16, and 17 (time code: 01:05:37-01:17:59) from *The Karate Kid*. Watch the clip and discuss Miyagi's patience and wisdom as well as Daniel's teachability, accompanied by his frustration and confusion. What might each have been thinking throughout the process?

When you first became a Christian, would you say that you felt as if you had "arrived," or as if you had "just begun"? Explain.

Has your answer changed through the years?

Messages from the King

Intelligence Briefing
What training did we receive when we
entered life at ground zero, with our
birthday suit on? It was like, ready or not
HERE'S LIFE! No wonder we wail
when life is spanked into us!
—John

According to chapter 12, what do I suggest is the purpose for Christian growth and training?

Does that differ from what you felt or have been taught in the past was its purpose?

How so?

> *We do not wage war as the world does. The weapons we fight with are not the weapons of the world. On the contrary, they have divine power to demolish strongholds.*
> *(2 Corinthians 10:3-4)*

On the top of page 126, I write: "But if the political machine, or big business, or the pimp on the street corner is the Enemy that you are fighting, you are fighting the wrong enemy."

What do you suppose I meant by this? Can you think of any modern examples?

I think that we would all agree that our source of strength for this battle is not in ourselves or our own plans, but only in Christ. Having said that then, where then do we begin our training?

Messages from the King

Intelligence Briefing12
It's that whole intentionally living thing that
gets us, isn't it? Generally speaking, we live
intentionally when we are born again and are
in crisis; but as a whole, we tend not to use the
weapons at our disposal for everyday living.
—Jim

Paul tells us that we "do not run like a man running aimlessly" and we "do not fight like a man beating the air" (1 Corinthians 9:26). What would be the difference in our walk with Christ if we approached this life with the training of a Navy Seal or the commitment of a marathon runner?

Scouting Report

Living in a relatively safe and peaceful nation, we have this natural tendency to look at the armor of God as optional. I own a number of swords. They are ornate, fun to "play" with, and honestly kind of cool; but I don't really need them . . .and I really don't know how to use them either. There is no reason to. It is very unlikely that I will ever be called upon to wield one of them. Unfortunately, many of us look at our spiritual armor in the same light. We love the way it looks, and occasionally we'll take it out to show it off, but we honestly doubt that it is a necessity.

Nothing could be further from the truth.

Let's start with the "belt of truth." What is it? Why do you think that it's the first piece of armor Paul mentions in Ephesians 6?

How do we train ourselves to wear this belt of truth?

What exactly is our breastplate?

A breastplate fits over the chest in order to protect the heart. How does our breastplate do that?

What is the danger of failing to recognize this and not "acquiring" this piece of armor?

Messages from the King

One of the oldest and deepest wounds inflicted upon me
growing up was the fact that my dad never closely mentored
me into manhood. He was always good about offering
me his advice, but it was seldom accompanied by practical
instruction. What I learned early on in life was that if I wanted
to learn how to do anything, I had to learn it do it myself.
Sadly, this is how I often see God.
—Allan

When Paul instructs us to fit our feet with the readiness of the gospel, he is telling us that we may be called on at any moment.

Can you identify a time in the battle that you did not have your feet fitted with readiness (that you were not trained or prepared to go at the moment you were needed)? Discuss.

The Theatre of the Round Table

Watch one more clip from *The Matrix*, chapter 36 (time code 02:01:41-02:05:36). It is the scene in which Neo literally holds up a shield of faith. Ask yourself a couple of questions: 1) Why did the bullets pierce him the first time? 2) What was the process of learning the truth about himself?

In this *Matrix* clip (above Theatre) what was the progression that Neo went through to forge that shield?

Do you think he could have done that at the very beginning of the movie? What are the analogies about how our shield is forged?

Messages from the King

Intelligence Briefing
God's timing with my calling has been a
major point of frustration for me, but when
I step back, I realize that it is clearly a
training and equipping season.
—Zachary

On the bottom of page 133, I state that "our helmet of salvation is our lifeline. It has saved us, it will save us, and it is saving us." Discuss your understanding of that statement—what it *has* saved us from, what it *will* save us from, and what our helmet *is* saving us from at this moment.

How do we appropriate or "put on" this helmet?

How easy do you think it was back in medieval times to learn to fight with a sword?
    What would it take for a knight to become proficient with its use?

In that light, what must we be doing with our sword (the Word of God) as we prepare for battle?

Prayer is at the very end of Paul's list as he describes arming ourselves. Speculate some on why he might have ended his discussion on the armor of God with this weapon.

Knightly Reading
Ephesians 6
Joshua 1

Messages from the King

Chapter 13
Casualties

We were in the very maelstrom of the battle. Men were falling every moment. The horrible noise was incessant and almost deafening. Except that my mind was absorbed in my duties, I do not know how I could have endured the strain.
—Lt. Frederick L. Hitchcock
132ⁿᵈ Pennsylvania, at Bloody Lane
September 17, 1862

The first time that I read this quote by Lt. Hitchcock, I shuddered. I have neither experienced the horror nor the honor of fighting and serving in a physical war, and I cannot begin to imagine what that would be like. This much I do know, though: none return from that experience without being forever and profoundly changed.

Likewise, we cannot pass through this life that Christ has called us into without similarly experiencing not just the glory of battle but many of the horrors as well: grieving over fallen comrades, the loss of innocence.

We all fear loss. Perhaps it would be good at the beginning of this chapter to just lay out there, in the light, what some of those things or people are that you fear losing in this fight that we have been called into.

Messages from the King

The reality of life, as well as this war, is that good men and women fall—or more specifically—are taken out. It is hard to watch on the big screen but even harder when it happens closer to home.

You too have stories: stories of good friends shot down in the midst of battle, of men and women whom you have known whose hearts were on fire for God, only to have the piercing arrows of the Evil One take them out, perhaps through tragedy, moral failure, or even death. Share one of those stories.

The Theatre of the Round Table

Watch the opening scene from *Saving Private Ryan*, if you dare, as the men are storming the beaches of Normandy on June 6, 1944. Another option is *City of Angels*, chapters 34 and 35 (time code 01:34:00 – 01:41:53), in which Seth, after giving up immortality in order to live in and experience this world, loses the one he gave it all up for.

Often when we see others either fall away from their faith or suddenly experience circumstances or wounds that keep them from pursuing the call of God on their lives, we find ourselves questioning our own faith, or even God. What was your reaction to the story that you wrote above?

Messages from the King

Intelligence Briefing

A casualty is a man blown to pieces, disintegrated, nothing left of him but a name on a war memorial.

—John Terraine

Peter writes that God is "patient with you, not wanting any to perish" (2 Peter 3:9). Now if God's will is not for us to fall, who do you suppose is at the heart of these casualties?

Okay, I think I know what you are thinking about now. You are arguing that the rich young man (or our friend for that matter) had free will: God had given him the honor of making his own choices, and he chose riches (or whatever) over God. You are right. We are not here to excuse the sinner but rather to understand the circumstances surrounding the sin.

What do you think are some of the arrows that our enemy might use to make the things of this world so enticing that a man or woman would turn their back on their King?

Read again the Parable of the Lost Son (Luke 15:11-32). Of all the failings of both the younger and the older son noted in that story, which ones did the Father address?

Why is that?

Messages from the King

One of the crucial pieces of the puzzle is that we "must learn to interpret the times with wisdom."

What are the risks to our own walk with God and our place in this adventure when we misinterpret the events that happen around us and decide that the battle is just too much for us?

Satan's presence and tactics in our world are similar to those of a terrorist group because he seeks to intimidate people and disrupt their lives.

Describe those similarities as well as how our response to him must be like our nation's response to the terrorists.

One of our greatest risks as the bullets keep flying and friends begin to fall is simply the matter of losing heart—of just throwing up our hands and crying uncle.

What specific things can we do so that we do not lose heart in the midst of casualties?

Knightly Reading
Joel 2
Psalm 142

Messages from the King

Go back to the question that we asked at the beginning of this chapter. Recall those whom you have seen fall—those who have stood by you but for whatever reason have been taken out of the battle.

Take those fallen comrades now before your King and entrust them to His care. Share your pain and your feelings openly with Him and then ask Him to give you the strength to honor their bravery, forgive their failings, and continue on in the fight that cost them so much.

Messages from the King

Intelligence Briefing
"Do not let their sacrifices be in vain."
This says it all.
—Jim

Chapter 14
Why

And the leaves of the tree are for the healing of the nations.
(Revelation 22:2)

Have you ever had a reality-check experience like the auto accident I described, in which you either did or could have lost something of immeasurable value?

In the midst of those types of crises, why do all of the "other" things in life that had seemed so important suddenly become so minor?

One of the mistakes that we can make as we begin to recognize and understand this "unseen war" is to forget the big picture and just focus on the battle. We look at the story unfolding before our eyes and forget the great story, or as one person put it, we miss the forest for the trees.

Why do you suppose that is?

Messages from the King

Have you ever had a time of great celebration and fun? I'm not talking about a church pot-luck; I mean a time of just totally letting loose and enjoying the moment. Unfortunately for many of us, those times may have occurred in our youth when our inhibitions were non-existent. Perhaps they happened before we came to Christ and learned to "control ourselves."

Forgiving and forgetting that period of immaturity and sin, what were those times like?

Describe what your ultimate celebration would look like.

Jesus promised that He was preparing a great banquet party just for us with shouting and singing and the finest clothes, where old friends and new ones will gather, and where "no one can take away your joy" (John 16:22). Share your thoughts about this. Are you looking forward to this day with anticipation, or are you dreading this day with a sense of trepidation?

How would you describe your emotions—as those of a young child awaiting Christmas morning, or more like those of a teenager being told that the family reunion will be "fun"?

What might be at the root of those sentiments?

Scouting Report

Satan has done such a good job of convincing us that heaven will be nothing more than an eternal church service, with no adventure, passion, relationships, or recreation. Nothing could be further from the truth. For an honest and thorough study of what the Scriptures say about our eternal home, I would highly recommend Randy Alcorn's book, Heaven.

Messages from the King

Let's go back again to the beginning of Jesus' ministry. In Luke 4, as He stands up in the temple and unrolls the scroll, He is explaining what it is that He has come to do. Listen:

> *"The Spirit of the Lord is on me, because he has*
> *anointed me to preach good news to the poor. He has*
> *sent me to proclaim freedom for the prisoners and*
> *recovery of sight for the blind, to release the oppressed,*
> *to proclaim the year of the Lord's favor"* (Luke 4:18-19).

Jesus came to set us free from the bondage of slavery—the slavery that has kept us from Him and the slavery that has been a result of these battles that we have fought. Why do you think it is important for us to remember that in the midst of the chaos of warfare?

Write out, in detail and in your own words, the transcendent cause that you are fighting for. You may not have absolute clarity regarding all of the details. That's okay, most of us don't. Just write out what you *do* know. Then stop and find a quiet place—a place away from the noise of life, away from your cell phone, away from the kids—and take a seat at the King's table. Ask your Father specifically what He has called you to. Ask Him what your "why" is. Write down any thoughts or impressions that come to mind. Ask Him to affirm or adjust what you had written earlier. Don't worry about the details, the improbabilities, or your lack of resources or talent. Just begin asking Him for your "why."

Knightly Reading

Revelation 19-22

Messages from the King

The Theatre of the Round Table
Watch chapter 57 from *The Lord of the Rings: The Return of the* King (time code: 02:53:09-02:57:59). That is *your* future and *your* destiny —to stand with your King. (No, I don't believe that Jesus will bow to us, but I do believe that we will receive honor and rule with Him, even to the point of judging angels [1 Corinthians 6:3].)

This study is ending, but *your life is just beginning*. The battle is upon us, and you are needed greatly. As we close out this study, I would encourage you to again go before your King and re-affirm to Him in your own words your love, your service, and your commitment to His Crown. Speak boldly with the authority that you have in Christ. If you are not sure what to pray, I have included a sample prayer. (But a word of warning: This prayer cannot just be read. You must speak it from your heart to both your King and your enemy).

And then, go.

Fight well, and be strong.

I will see you on the battlefield.

Messages from the King

Intelligence Briefing

If we can but hold a picture of what lies ahead of us on the other side of eternity, throughout the rest of our days that are gifted to us here on earth we can fittingly say, "It will be worth it all." Our King's party awaits us.

—John

135

Father, my King, I come before You now, to Your table, to take my rightful place as Your heir, claiming all that Christ accomplished for Me in His sufferings, His death, His resurrection, and His ascension. I put to death my old self and all that was attached to it. I agree with You that Jesus' sacrifice was sufficient, and I accept as true my new self holy and righteous in Christ. I reject the lie of my enemy that says I must in any way add to the perfect sacrifice of my Lord Jesus.

Now, by the authority of Christ that has been given to me, I declare to my enemy, Satan and all foul spirits, that they no longer have any claim to me or anything that is in my domain. Here, I draw a line in the sand and remind those who would minister evil that "greater is He who is in me than He who is in the world." I command them, by this authority of Christ, to flee from me and from all that is mine.

In their place now, I invite my Lord to again take up residence. I confess those places that I have compromised my faith, laid down my armor, or surrendered my sword. I invite the finished and full work of Christ into my life.

And now I offer to my King my service. Teach me to fight, wield a sword, stay in the battle, and walk in faith. Train me in the ways of Your kingdom, and may that kingdom permeate my very being. Give me eyes to see and ears to hear. Teach me wisdom and discernment, bring fellow warriors into my court, and fully complete the good work that You have begun in me.

Here today, I commit myself to this battle and look forward to the return of my King, to whom I offer all praise and all honor, and in whose name I boldly pray,

Amen.

Messages from the King

About the Author

David Kortje is an author, speaker, and motivator whose heart is to see the children of God walk in all the fullness of Life that Christ has for us.

David has carried his message of freedom in Christ to numerous churches, para-church organizations, and ministries throughout the United States. He is the director and founder of **Knight Vision Ministries**.

Giving his life to Christ in 1987 while in Medical School, David has spent the last 21 years in Christian ministry, leading small groups, preaching and teaching, leading retreats and conference speaking, while also practicing medicine full time.

David received a Bachelor of Science Degree, Summa Cum Laude, from the University of Nebraska Omaha, and his M.D. from the University of Nebraska Medical Center. His experience as a physician has greatly influenced his desire to see people healed emotionally as well as spiritually.

David has written numerous newsletter and journal articles, has a weekly blog, and is the author of *The Unseen War, Winning the Fight for Life* (Parson Place Press, 2009).

Husband of 25 years to Sandra, and a father of four, David loves backpacking, rock climbing and racing motocross in his free time.

He is available for speaking engagements through his website: www.knightvisionministries.com. There you will also find additional resources as well as his personal blog to further assist you in winning this fight for *life*.